THE EDUCATION OF DESIRE

This book was supported
by a grant from the
Eric Mathieu King Fund
of the Academy
of American Poets.

WESLEYAN POETRY

WILLIAM DICKEY

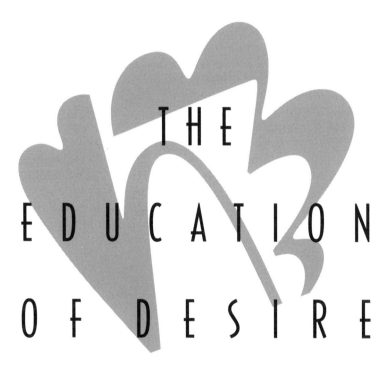

THE EDUCATION OF DESIRE

WESLEYAN UNIVERSITY PRESS

Published by University Press of New England / Hanover and London

Wesleyan University Press

University Press of New England, Hanover, NH 03755

© 1996 by The Estate of William Dickey

All rights reserved

Printed in the United States of America

5 4 3 2 1

CIP data appear at the end of the book

The publisher gratefully acknowledges the support of
Lannan Foundation in the publication of this book.

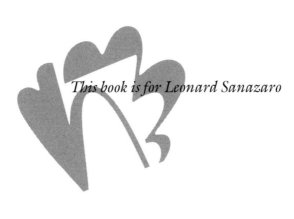

This book is for Leonard Sanazaro

Listen. Remember how it was with the

acrobats. Watch them carefully, hear

the least word, especially what they say

to one another, in another language—-

don't let them escape you; it's the only

time for hallucination, the last time.

They can't stay. They'll be somewhere

else this time tomorrow.

—EUDORA WELTY

Powerhouse

CONTENTS

FOREWORD

By W. D. Snodgrass

"He was so old when he was young and so young when he was old," said Clark Blaise about his former teacher, William Dickey. When I knew Bill as a fellow student, some years earlier at the University of Iowa, he always seemed half-cramped by what I took for arthritis (actually the result of a back injury from a fall while a student at Reed College). His manner seemed donnish, superior but warmly amused, droll and friendly but bent under the weight of bookish learning. He was laboring toward a PhD in creative writing and married to a psychiatric nurse. On the wall of Clark Blaise's office as director of the International Writers' Program in Iowa City, there still hangs a photo of a mock funeral held at Kenny's Bar. (then the favorite hangout for Workshop students); the young man lying in the coffin is, of course, Bill Dickey.

Of this later manner, after he'd emerged from several closets, I will report only that various friends disagree about whether he had dyed his hair on both head and chest orange or auburn. The more important point is that these poems, written at the end of his life and with his death of AIDS clearly in sight, are a young man's poems. Having chosen Dickey's first book, *Of the Festivity*, for the Yale Series of Young Poets in 1959, W. H. Auden credited it with three necessary virtues: "the lines speak, something has been noticed, and speech and observation have become the servants of a personal vision." As he sees it, "Mr. Dickey's specialty is nightmare worlds described in the simplest possible diction."

Yet if we look at the poems of the first book—say, at a few lines from the title poem, "Of the Festivity"

> Afraid of words, the tenderness of words
> That come to the lips out of their own accord—
> Here peace must marry with the violent sword,
> Its violence collected to repose,

and compare them with a few lines from "Danaë" in his last book

> Not what the *lumpenprolatariat* arrives at nightly
> interjection of a gross member into a tin receptacle . . .
>
> buttock and balls grammar, the loud graffiti . . .
>
> I sublimed him in the virginal juices of my body
>
> transparent to what runs from a perfectly roasted chicken
> into spendable income, into a medium of exchange
>
> by which I mean not the thing but its abstract
> not the foot but podiatry, . . .

this sounds less like the Theban elders creaking out to Dionysus' festivity than like Dionysus himself. Not only the diction, but the leaps of ideas and image, the levels of language, the movement of the line all seem younger, incredibly more vigorous. This is neither to slight the traditional metre of the first book nor to ignore the marvelous tenderness of the early poem. It is to point out the new poem's wild prankiness, the giddy whirl of idea and vision. This is like doing nude cartwheels in the snow (the way the younger man injured his back).

Kathrine Varnes, his student late in his career, writes, "The quality of his work that I like the most is his ability to say very risky things while laughing." That ability dominates "The Metamorphoses," the new book's first section. Here, Dickey draws heavily on Ovid, yet also holds his own imminent death (and metamorphosis) in sight. Throughout, the key idea is edge, frontier, periphery—that which marks the border between states of being; the constant urge is to live as near as possible to that edge, the limit that marks a transformation. Danaë, a western gunslinger, the Virgin Mary, Little Red Riding Hood, Sir Lancelot, Tiresias, a lemming-like tribe, the Monarch butterfly—one after another are transformed from physical existence, from blood and "provocative butts," into idea. That transformation is always performed by the observer's "individual eyes":

> The collection of bananas intent on its randomness

arguing nothing, arrives over and over
at significant form as an eye individuates.

So the physical, its details and oppositions, is transfigured by the observer's (and especially the artist's) eye and brain. And that transformation—as in the superscript from Eudora Welty, "It's the last chance for hallucination"—is to be sought and cherished. The second section, "The Bone Pit," deals, expectably, with death—with the nightmare world of Auden's remark. After the initial poem, "The Arrival of the Titanic" (Dickey's response to the AIDS epidemic), these poems are less often concerned with physical death and destruction than with the spiritual death and the pseudo-life of our culture, with physical reality untransformed. Here the rich old woman chants

> I go Tiffany, Cartier, Harry Winston.
> I go Saks, I go Peck and Peck . . .

the Cardinal chants

> Bare-chested boys in their Levis, I love to see
> their nakedness tarnish . . .

the President of the United States chants

> I go out into the world naked with my leashed dogs.
> My dogs are three in number. Their names are Power . . .
> There is no dish other than the dish we eat from.

Here, the Troll King (a.k.a. Mattias von und zu Abendstern) absent-mindedly injects zoo sounds into his night club act winning ovations from his beastly audience as well as, apparently, the Nobel Prize. But this also is the world of the AIDS ward with its BLOOD PRECAUTIONS sign, its recovery of mere physical existence where no overseeing eye provides order, where "he" or "she" is retrieved alone beyond the union of any "they," where only the passing breath gives evidence of life.

"The Education of Desire" is the title not only of the book but also of its third section and of the final cycle of twelve poems. This third section opens with two poems rejecting both attraction to and repulsion against the merely physical: "My Sweet Undertaker" and "The Death of John Berryman." These are followed by two poems about the satisfied and satisfying mature relationship, "Roses" and "Evening," then by the poems of the title sequence.

Allen Mandelbaum's translation of the *Purgatorio* has Virgil state that "love is the seed in you of every virtue and of all acts deserving punishment." Mandelbaum continues, in his commentary, "To find the same source for all good and all evil is to insist on the need for the education of desire." Love, then, is the central theme of all the poems in this book and of all their problems of boundaries, of memory, of suffering. In this last section we are surprised to find several simple, lucid, and direct poems quite outside the hallucinatory, half-surreal techniques, the wrenched syntax and language of the earlier poems, yet coming as a sort of resolution and consolation for the problems there raised. Particularly lovely are the already mentioned "Roses," the exquisite gift-lyric "Earthquake, Volcano," and, above all, the final superb lyric, crystal clear yet charged with mystery:

> On the white road
> in dust of summer
> someone's arriving

Who is this "clothed only in light . . . his eyes full of islands/stroked by blue ocean/in the summer air"? The young Dionysus? Whitman's wayfaring lover-divinity? The transfigured Death? Who's to deny any of them or deny them all as one? That, though, would be a miracle, wouldn't it? (And what else should a poem be?)

Kathrine Varnes writes, "I like the way the poems don't expect me to applaud them for having a feeling as much as they seem to show thinking through the feelings." I don't think that could be better said. Nor could that poem.

San Miguel de Allende, Mexico
February 1996

I

THE METAMORPHOSES

The Metamorphoses

1. Tribe from the Interior

sea-seeking, the rumor of sea, not an idea
it has had before, in the shadow of the great trees

inches its way, many times the flayed skin tents
erected and taken down, red infants sacrificed

to the half-formed mask of the journey, journeying
out from the world's belly and clotted private parts

all it knows of itself, towards where,
if the drenched shag of the menstrual wood relents

it will find itself one morning in an edge of fog
and under its sudden foot nothing, cliff, live

drop to the otherness of the unresisting water
a blow of beyond unshelling their individual eyes

2. *Danaë*

Not what the lumpenproletariat arrives at nightly:
interjection of a gross member into a tin receptacle

but if I thought of it carefully it would convert,
high art out of the common comic strip, the

buttock and balls grammar, the loud graffiti
he was agreeable saying "anything

you want, I am fluid with restlessness"
I sublimed him in the virginal juices of my body

transparent as what runs from a perfectly-roasted chicken
into spendable income, into a medium of exchange

by which I mean not the thing but its abstract
not the foot but podiatry, not the slippery mouth

pushing and squirming to deform the ellipse of my breast
but a science of nutrition. He had not known

intellectually what it was like to be a god before
and as the shower of gold whitened and lessened

willingly he took back into himself the apparatus of touch
unblooded as myth, an intimate of horizons

3. The Idea of the Frontier

> The red of the grass made all the great prairie the colour
> of wine-stains, or of certain seaweeds when they are first
> washed up. And there was so much motion in it; the
> whole country seemed, somehow, to be running.
> —Willa Cather, *My Ántonia*

Put on his hat, took out his six-shooter, bang
a domino row of villains, stretching out over

the end of the street to what was beyond the set
fell down; techs struck the canvas, plucked

the blond sun down out of his hairs of sky
into jurisdiction; nobody felt any better

but the whole wagon train rooted where it had been moving
the horses put down roots, babies grew button-down collars

mothers began to whisper Internal Revenue
they had come to the edge and by their arrival there

it had ceased to be; anywhere now
lead back rather than forward; indignant buzzards

froze, two-dimensional, onto the eight-foot ceiling
infinitives replaced participles, nobody,

nothing was running, nothing was happening anywhere
except at night, in the seacaves of anxiety dreams

4. *What Took Place in the Wood*

First Little Red Ridinghood met the wolf
and was much attracted by his spats and platinum watch chain

and after they were married she bore twins and again twins
a boy human and a girl wolf and then the opposite

naming them Arizona Colorado New Mexico and Utah
for four states that exactly converged

they grew up and married each other because how were they to
know
there was anything different? the children of incest

became a race of lovable retarded gods
playing with toy railroads and when collisions came

accidental or manufactured the people inside the parlor cars
were too small for blood and blood gathered itself up

and went away into the uncertain light at morning and evening
promising nothing about a time or about a language of return

5. *Amazonas*

Great-branching venous and capillary marrying rivers
shape of a tree root and apex outside the eye

everything speaking its own language and not understood
the men not understood by the women and vice-versa

each child speaking of itself only by the private name
it found on a path in the rain forest where the path ended

as many kinds of animals as there could be
ideas of animals either by thinking of them

or by their thinking of themselves, plenitude
the theological doctrine under which God created

everything that could possibly exist as continuous
so that one more thing is always being created

and comes into a dangerous world as a new danger
a jade jaguar, an unjade jaguar, a gold jaguar

a jaguar that cannot be understood as such, a jaguar God
that from any point you place him draws multiple

images from that point to every other point
is never satisfied because satisfaction assumes

the possibility of death, and here there are only jaguars
being born, and everything not a jaguar or a river being born also

6. *"Had I Been the Virgin Mary I Would Have Said No"*

A difficult problem in anatomy: how to attach wings
to the shoulder blades of humans and make them look workable

either the wings or the humans; carrying a tin trumpet
and accompanied by a minstrel band that used to tour the South

in the days before the germ theory had been discovered
Gabriel shuffles in to make this one-time limited offer

in an early illumination Mary is assumed into heaven
by the agency of a sky-blue openwork elevator cage

it does take careful thought; what is it about gods
that insists on making more gods out of human beings

crucifying them as one pits a peach, to release the seed?
what is it about the human imagination that insists on being used

by anybody in a beat-up 1936 Chevy with bruised fenders
selling Old Doctor Barmecide's indigestion powders

or demands the harsh ruffle of painfully-extended wings
pulling the back muscles out of true, demands

grace, as if without the mysterious secret ingredient
Mary was not yet Mary, only an opportunity?

7. *Moons*

At the Methodist ice cream sociable they meet
he in a hot straw hat, she in her dusk-colored skirts

that in a corner of the night begin unfolding.
A principle is established: a thing like a tiny dot

in the center of a piece of virgin paper
begins unfolding, doubles and lies flat

panting with the effort, doubles itself again.
Nothing is involved that we could call

Consciousness, any more than in the automatic
opening of an umbrella that continues opening.

The ice cream sociable continues, growing older
and less distinct under a succession of moons

the rain moon, the hunter's moon, the burial moon,
the moon of replacement. Something has opened

and continues opening, gradually using up the future
which turns out to be all of the space there is.

8. The Quest for the Holy Grail

Having kept himself perfectly pure, in the face of
temptations from choruses of dance-hall girls

wiggling their provocative butts, the more obscure temptations
of the defrocked priest practicing Shiatsu massage

having passed through the wilderness of Pachinko parlors
and the other wilderness of art for art's sake

he arrives at the eroded steps of the castle
perfectly stilled. No one is there to welcome him.

This is not a place of welcome, but of obliteration.
He enters the indifferent hall and achieves the Grail

which is a flat dull dish of common pewter,
unmarked. He raises it to his lips

for the ritual kiss. At the sound of his lips kissing
the lights in the castle go out, a small wind

whispers through the corridors, the voices
of generation dying down the blind flights of stairs.

9. *The Egoist*

Popped from the womb, he began gathering property
extorted from his wet nurses by threatening

to turn blue in the face and die. Everyone gave in.
His mother dressed him in guava-colored lace crinolines

his father obligingly retired to the *Côte d'Azur*
siblings were disposed of by the Beast of the Bassinet.

Coextensive with the world, his hands become The Hands,
his mouth The Mouth, his dingus The Dingus.

Absolute power corrupts absolutely said Lord Acton.
Absolute corruption set in: a foot revolted

and proclaimed democracy and universal male suffrage
the hairs of his armpit began drinking heavily

and all over his body an asexual budding
produced nodes of himself, his genetic encumberment

replicated and replicated, an oblique hysteria.
The absolute corruption of self is community.

The absolute corruption of the mouth
is to taste its tongue over and over, to be continually filled.

10. *Life Study*

Rameses erases all of the inscriptions
on the obelisks that are pre-Rameses

and applies himself to the glorification of his own name.
We all do that: taking out and replacing bookplates

that said wistfully *Methuselah His Book*
or *Ozymandias, Librarian of Librarians.*

The placid young woman curled into a double cube
on the posing couch a vessel from which is taken

one affirmation after another and remains instilled.
The collection of bananas intent on its randomness

arguing nothing, arrives over and over
at significant form as an eye individuates

the electric turbine develops under scrutiny
powerful thighs and an intention. Were you

a lesson before I began to read you? Were you
a where waiting for its temporary when?

11. *David Dances Before Saul*

Eccentric cymbals, a stutter of nose-flutes,
the geometric complications of Bokhara carpets

laid over the prevailing dust, sellers of ripe figs
in the shadow of the camels' monumental disdain,

a confusion of legs and breasts, generic nipples
at its equator, oiled hair out to the unknown peripheries.

It is everything the king possesses and must try to rule.
David takes off his hat and stands motionless

cigarette in the corner of his mouth, his eyes squinted
against the curl of the smoke, a flat hand

cuts with a sardonic gesture, dismissing.
Suddenly there is no one but David in the king's eye

the effect of minimalism. The dance is over.
It had such focus it did not need to begin.

12. *The Election of the Empress of San Francisco*

Down from a swing in the rafters descends Michelle
who has been freezing her buns off up there

she says, taking the microphone, touching up
with the tip of her little finger her mascara

as before her the night flowers begin to unleash
their petals, the chartered professional accountants

of the multiple desks of noon undo their names.
A beguine enters and shivers through the cold theatre

as the candidates for conversion, the born one way
elaborate themselves, forcing a cleavage

Diana surrounded by naked huntsmen, leopards
striding through muscular episodes of flowers

the caught spume of the Mediterranean wave
hovering as breath hangs in between slabs of air

a thread, a narrow aperture that allows.
The winner, says Michelle, before she is hoisted

by the sweat of a million agreements, back up into
a chilly waiting space paid for by the unanimous sky.

13. *The Weather of This World*

I came into the map by the left entrance, the one
with all the puffy-cheeked gods blowing winds

and the inscription *Hic sunt dracones*
where, before birth, everything lies undiscovered

Now it is time to go; the retirement specialist
sets a very small fire in the center of the known world

and without blazing, or much smoke in the hazy sunlight
it chars outward; the conventional symbols for rivers

are eaten back toward their source in the high mountains
the magical unlivable cities gather their trim suburbs

into an eroded stillness, bird song,
even the low unending metre of the night

slips up out of hearing, the bound scores
of late Beethoven quartets, the dog barking at morning

what was it like, when the seasons
turned their decorated wheel over and over across the sky?

when the archer, sign of my birth, half horse, half human,
reconciles his nature, and lays down the tensed bow?

14. *Argument*

> Her face had a kind of fascination for me: it was the very
> colour and shape of anger.
>
> —Willa Cather, *My Ántonia*

She gathered up anger in a basket, where it grew
wild as a berry in the sand of the low hills

or she harvested it from the sea in a long net
woven from the hair of the dead; anger was

the yeast in the bread she baked, what made her claws
scissor the back of her lover in the little death

as light fills with itself, as the transparent wine bottle
becomes only the vehicle for what it contains

she turned herself into anger, her bones reddened
with a bramble fire of wreathed and engorging veins

and night sat down on her like the lid of an iron kettle
holding itself in and in, not a taste escaping

15. *And I Tiresias Have Experienced All*

This beggar with the empty eye-sockets was man and woman
as the day dictated: either he was hairy and full of beer

and cruised down Mission Street in a low-rider
belching, propositioning policewomen, or else she was

stationed in her neon shorts with the shaved crotch
hustling the annual convention of the AMA

or else he was eighteen, thin, depilating his chest
while she tried strapping on the cold rubber dildo

or else she married herself in the orange blossoms
of the difficult South, or else he heard

in a Honolulu bar the voice of his mother whisper
and took her tongue into his mouth in desecration

or else they stopped and refused, their faces frozen
in the white glare of the autopsy, and their names flew

out the window of the Hall of Justice and were lost
in a wood rustling with unexpected children

16. The Birthmark of the World on the World's Forehead

My totem animal is the mouse deer; I was born
in the Year of Repentance when the yellow floods came

and swept away the amusement pier; I cut my nails
by moonlight and locked up the curved parings.

Generosity was not my meat. The bewitched soprano
hoping against hope she can make it to C over *alt*

or the lungfish burrowing down as the drought strengthens:
I carry their signs in my mind, and the mind shows

narrow and indignant through the flaky skull
as in early arithmetic lessons: the computer spins

long into the night trying to divide by zero
and the spider given LSD loses the web's pattern.

17. *In the Guano Islands*

The forms to be filled out in detail, the blue form
is your history of arrests and humiliations, the pink form

how many times you have drawn blood in your career
as a female anopheles mosquito, the buff form

where you were caught with your pants down shitting
in the tin underbrush outside the company picnic

all of the other forms (puce, carnelian)
instances of your unworthiness to be chosen

for permanent employment in the guano islands
by the guano corporation whose guano executives

pile up one over another under the decomposing
very low tropical sky until the top and the bottom

meet with a lead clank and you are flattened between them
on a part-time basis without health benefits

or social security, but you are grateful as always
to be demoted to darkness, even when

there is no classification to be demoted into.

18. *Monarch Butterflies*

The most unfolded thing, before and after
nothing to do with each other, as if out of

a gravel streambed at the pale glacier's foot
light bell-note of water against ice at the break of winter

a forest of tree ferns blazed up and luxurious
epiphytes perfumed the over-laden branches.

A short voice in hiding, a concentration
of idea in containment, a banked fire

what most under pressure most appreciates
the expansion of flight, what most

monochromatic and burned and drab anticipates
the explosion of distance upholding its intense wings.

The Hour between Dog and Wolf

No one has anything to do with me any more, now that I have come to live in this hour, which is neither one thing nor the other. I was a prosperous merchant in the seaport of L___; I married young and had children, and they still exist, or I can persuade myself that they exist, but they are in clock time, where washing day is the first day of the week, and meals are prepared and eaten.

My mother was a believer in ghosts. As she grew older, she became a kind of ghost herself: at least it was their world rather than mine that she chose to live in. She liked the insubstantial; it hurt her less, and everything the day presented to her hurt her; she had that expectation and that capacity. She told me stories about ghosts and their invulnerability: how a sword passes through them without drawing blood.

As a game, then, or at the beginning as a game, I thought of myself as becoming invisible. Does any of us like the body he walks around in, with all of its animal functions and its premises of decay? In the public baths I would look at my white legs and feet, and wish they were furniture or the pedestals of machines, that I had not to take care of them and worry about their deliberate changing.

The great artists, the great rhetoricians, walking and arguing with their students in the square before the library, they are allowed to arrive at new places in their minds: the flutter of a corner of a handkerchief becomes the sail of a vessel coasting a colored shore in the Spice Islands, or they can form themselves so geometrically that their bodies are thought into many-sided crystals, which fall to the ground and can be picked up and saved.

I went to many doors in my dissatisfaction. Most of them were closed against me, but I found the door into the root cellar, where the massive winter vegetables lie and boast to one another and seek to grow heavier, and the minute door, at the top left corner of a closed window, into the fly trap, where the common houseflies persecuted and revered a moth that had joined them. I found doors into cheese and butter, a door into paper, both written upon and not, a door into recurrent fever.

How am I to describe this place, here, to you, except to say that in it everything wants to be and does not find being very possible? How terrible to be caught in the middle of a transformation and ever afterwards to exist with the chest and belly of a snake, and the crowned illuminated head of an archangel.

It is flat, mostly. It never rises into hills where you are, but only in the distance, and they are not hills confident enough in themselves to appear as landscape. The buildings are, not to put too fine a term upon it, huts, made out of straw and dung and the leaves of discarded books and pieces of toys children have thrown away: the little wheels could be thought of as eyes if anyone could imagine a face to contain them. Nothing is very like anything else; it is hard even to try to form connections.

The hour—you can understand that—is always twilight, between understandings. Kings have been ruling and doing justice up until this time, and now their power is expended. A different kind of power will come into possession of itself soon: priestesses with their white birds flying around them, and the god speaking to them out of their bellies. But I have no idea when soon is.

It may be enough for me that my beard no longer grows and has to be shaved away, that my penis no longer hardens of itself in the night and noses about it. There are things I am glad to have dispensed with, like digestion. But a moral lesson cannot consist only of its first step: the giving away. I was supposed to have been allowed some edge in return—the eclipse's edge, cutting the face of the moon.

Many times in my life I wished to be disencumbered, made into an obedience to some powerful and bitter command exterior to me. I grew shorter as I grew older; there may be a pattern of unintention working in that. Even the leaves have skeletons; look at the bare ribs underlying them and you can see they are like patterns of weak fingers.

What I am going to do now is to walk toward the hills, and see whether, if I walk long enough, the hills will decide to let me arrive there. I think there are wild beasts among them, all kinds of predators: grave lions and witty tormenting foxes. I think that after the twilight they must gather around a water hole and look dangerously at one another, and play at killing.

This hour some have supposed to be magic: to have in it possibilities of a sacred double soul, not higher or lower, merely different. I can tell you it is not worth coming here to discover whether those stories are true.

THE BONE PIT

The Arrival of the *Titanic*

Gashed, from her long immobility on the sea-bed
gravid with the dreams of invertebrates, only half
here in the sense of consciousness, she pulls,
grey on a grey morning into New York Harbor,
bearing all of the dead in their attitudes, the old dead
in dinner jackets, bare feet encrusted with barnacles,
their pearls eyes, their old assurance of conquest
over the negligent elements, and walking thin and
perplexed among them the new dead who
never realized on what crossing they had embarked.

We are the photograph's negative, made after
the color print, made after the abyssal waters
took color out of the Liberty scarves, the bright
upper atmosphere of tea dances, after the drift
downward, the pressures of winter. If it has been
abandoned, it is ours, it comes sailing silently
back with us. There were never enough
lifeboats, and never
enough gaiety to see us safely through past moonrise
and our monochrome exploration into the range of ice.

Plum

Now the plum blossom on its Chinese branch
argues in spring across the waterless country.
Spring as a fist. Its delicacies clench.

So it is in time of war as the bench-
marks of the bodies build & the fluid gentry
paint artificial plums onto the stiff branch

dowsing for oil and vinegar in the trench-
works, forcing their unlubricated entry,
a fist in spring & the bruised membranes clench

& convulse under the violating drench
of fire & the tight flayed missile gantry
flings the fire's blossom from its bitter branch.

Body the beggar in the chemical launch
upward, body the zero into which the wintry
spring comes as a fist to couple its dead clench

body the rotted petal, the death-stench
covering the feet of the rigid erected sentry,
the fingers of the plum blossom, crisping, clench
for the branch, for the branch's buried country.

The Frog Footman and the Fish Footman

Aiee! It is the ceremony of the first blades of winter.
Horticulture, horticulture, the little steam train says puffing up
    the mountainside.
As if he had never known a home of his own, only ditches.
Three stomps with a stone stump and the colloquium started.
Beggars under the drainpipe, another hand's cast of the bone
    dice.
Whatever name the event has, it can be understood as an invita-
    tion.
Epilepsy, epilepsy, the little steam train said, descending at
    evening.
They bowed so low that their wigs tangled and I had to laugh.

Chants

1. *The Rich Old Woman*

I go Tiffany, Cartier, Harry Winston.
I go Saks, I go Peck & Peck, I go
white toothless ghost Abercrombie & Fitch.
I wave ceremonial credit card, I spend money.
We all eat, we all eat the quiche, the fondue.
We all eat the red heart out of the opera.
Hammacher Schlemmer, we cry, Hammacher Schlemmer.

2. *The Conservative Supreme Court Justice*

Every morning my shoes shined by the house slave.
Every morning my meat served by the meat slave.
Every morning the slave for sewing sews on
my face, my fists, my heavy white genitals.
When the slaves are through I breathe, I speak, I am ready.

Every evening I count in my cell for counting.
Every evening the woman aborts on the red table.
Every evening I sing, I grow younger and younger.
I count the number of blood
the number of the stained thighs.

3. *The Leader of the Aryan Nation*

In my kitchen there is a drum drumming.
In my bathroom there is a drum drumming.
In my bedroom there is a drum drumming.
The drumheads are made of the belly skins of the unworthy.
The drumheads are all colors, belly colors of the unworthy.
I hit the drumheads, they drum to my music.
I hit the drumheads with my drumsticks of picked bone.

30

4. *The Cardinal*

The women barefoot and pregnant, I love to see
the women barefoot and pregnant, the young girls,
just as they reach for the flower, cut into renunciation.

Bare-chested boys in their Levis, I love to see
their nakedness tarnish, the shirt of exasperation
poison the skin until all of the skin itches.

Dead and unborn, unformed, I love to see,
rosaries in their throats, strangle of beads
stilling the slim voices of the merely living.

5. *The Lumber Company Executive*

The sacred direction: down. Bring it to down.
Bring down these tents of assertion, the enemy,
the tall ones.

The sacred color: red. Bring it to red.
Wash down the widening gorges of earth flesh
till the stone stiffens.

The sacred instrument, fire. Bring it to fire.
Fire's afterbirth, the long dangle of waste, pitted
by unwilling waters.

6. *The Critic*

I unscrewed the lip from the mouth, the mouth I discarded.
I unscrewed the lid from the eye, the eye I discarded.
Here is a doll made from pieces. The pieces hate one another.
Here are the doll and I in a posed photograph.
After the photograph was taken, I unscrewed the camera.

7. *The National Rifle Association Member*

This hide is a bear. I shot the hide sleeping.
This hide is a lion. I shot the hide mating.
This hide is an elephant. I shot the hide thinking.

I put on all of the hides and my many wives caress me.
I sleep, I mate, I think. Under the hides
I am a blue steel barrel empty with death.
This hide is a bird. I shot the hide flying.

8. *The President of the United States of America*

I go out into the world naked with my leashed dogs.
My dogs are three in number. Their names are Power.
They have been carefully trained to destroy the lesser.

Power over beggars destroys beggars. There are no beggars.
Power over deviants destroys deviants. There are no deviants.
Power over complaint destroys complaint. There is no complaint.

My dogs and I eat from the same dish and are satisfied.
There is no dish other than the dish we eat from.

Bungee Jumping

Aunt Mildred tied up her petticoats with binder's
twine, and my great-uncle Ezekiel waxed and waxed
his moustaches into flexibility. It was the whole
family off then into the dangerous continent of air

and while the salesman with the one gold eyetooth told us
the cords at our ankles were guaranteed to stretch
to their utmost and then bring us safely back
to the fried chicken and scalloped potatoes of Sunday dinner

nobody quite believed. Edwina, my father's half sister
by my grandfather's marriage to a former dance hall girl,
who got her doctorate in tensor evaluation, she said
whole galaxies have been known to belch and disappear

taking with them the King Charles spaniels and the gold-
plated fire hydrants from where the fire finally stopped
in the earthquake year. But it was no good growing
roots into the vegetable garden, not after the Monarch

butterflies flew up into one whirling vortex and blanked
out of immediate space, it was no good
hoping Ken and Barbie, sexless, would anchor us
to our interchangeable faces, or that our feet

those flat independent anemones, could grip forever.
The salesman smiled, with his face the size
of the Empire State and growing bigger and bigger
and into and through the face Aunt Mildred went

shouting "Banzai!" into Great-Uncle Ezekiel's
inherited ear trumpet, shredding it to tin ribbons,
and Edwina, dressed in the full commencement robes
of the University of Massachusetts at Amherst, and

Mother and Father wrapped in each other's
reminiscences, and the goldfish, and finally I went
too, out of the mold my body had been formed in
and inhabited, as if place were the only realization of person

and either the cords snapped, as any sceptic might have expected,
or they are stretched out finer than a human hair,
that keeps growing after death, even in the black melting
that may or may not be the tight coral beach beyond.

The Troll King

Matthias von und zu Abendstern had dropped his titles of nobility, reaching back behind him into the cloudy historicities of the Holy Roman Empire, when, out of financial necessity, he became a nightclub jazz singer in Hamburg in the difficult period between the wars. He was a young man without a future, too young to have served as a cavalry officer—the only chord his family connection could have heard in him—in a succession of lost campaigns, too broadly and impractically educated to succeed in any ordinary course of business, too sceptical of the validity of authority, whose worthlessness he recognized in others as in himself, to become a priest. Little was left, in the world as it then was, for him to do but to engage himself as a public entertainer.

The club in which he began his long career was located on an indifferent street in the old neighborhood of the Inner Harbor, and called itself, in an effort to borrow the cosmopolitan sophistication for which Berlin had at that time become legendary, Chez Poliphile. There, in a room no more than ten meters square, and crowded with minute tables, The Troll King, as he had elected to be known in the active but despairing world of the night, sang from a stage no higher than a footstool, accompanied by the only musicians the club's proprietors could afford, an epicene drummer addicted to cocaine, and two elderly sisters, who played, respectively, the flute and the saxophone. Though they had names, The Troll King, when he addressed them at all, spoke to them as Sister One and Sister Two.

The early childhood of von und zu Abendstern had been spent on the extensive country estate of his grandparents, who maintained not only a staff of thirty household servants, but also that educational toy of the aristocracy, a private zoo. The Troll King's success as a singer began one evening when, wearied of the uniformity and bleakness of imported American blues, inadequately translated into German, he permitted his mind to wander back into happier times, and found himself introducing into his performance the mating cry of a water bittern. It was all done without calculation, and perhaps on that account awoke in his slight audience a tremor of interest. In the small hours of the morning, as they packed away their instruments, Sisters One and Two congratulated The Troll King on his brief experiment. Even the debauched drummer glanced at him with surly respect, before slouching out into the dark streets in search of more cocaine.

From that first almost accidental epiphany arose The Troll King's eventual repertory, so moving to the lost spirits of his society, of jazz songs rendered in the various voices of the animal creation. In the beginning, modest of his abilities and given more to imitate than to invent, he confined himself to birds, but even here, the sureness of his artistic confidence growing, he steadily undertook more taxing impersonations, as, that of an Egyptian ibis at dawn by the cataracts of the upper Nile, or, his particular triumph in this earliest definition of his genre, the haunting and diminishing cry of a Darwin's rhea facing extinction. It was at this point in his career that The Troll King identified, one gratifying evening, a member of his audience as the already distinguished ornithologist, Konrad Lorenz, whose eyes, even in the smoky atmosphere of the nightclub, could be seen as glistening with appreciative tears.

For the artist, the only fatality is to repeat himself, and great success did not corrupt, as it so often does, The Troll King's vision. While sentimentalists in his audience cried out drunkenly for voices with which they had come to identify their own spent lives, the water bittern, the vole, the variegated thrush, The Troll King moved, with graceful dissonance, into the fugal complexities of the mammalian jungle; it was said by critics, of one of his first adventures in this canon, that as his voice took on the haunted twitterings of the lemur of Madagascar, it was possible to watch his eyes enlarge fifty-fold and become noctiluminescent, and the ends of his fingers turn spatulate, as if gripping with elastic assurance some alien branch.

The courts of Europe could still be said, barely, to exist, and before them The Troll King and his companions performed, as they performed, to wilder and wilder recognition, in the music halls of London, the Cirque d'Hiver in Paris, the old, lamented

36

Hippodrome of New York City. All of the members of the group prospered: Sister One had made for herself a flute in sterling silver, while Sister Two, the younger and more worldly, speculated in grain futures. Even the drummer could look at himself in the mirrors of grand hotels, a little in love with the elegance of his emaciation.

And so it went, until The Troll King began, to the disquiet and rancorous criticism of the entire world of musical art, that series of creations which led, it is not too much to say, to his apotheosis. He had exhausted, one by one, the voices, the imaginative capacities, of the lesser primates. It was a time of discovery in the researches of anthropology; The Troll King, studious always of the dead as well as the living, began to reconstruct, voice after non-existent voice, the ascent of man. Riots broke out in the Paris theatre which saw the première of his Neanderthaler, a guttural reminiscence of St. James Infirmary like the miasma of communal burying grounds whispering behind him. Peking Man, Cro-Magnon, from these he moved to the beginnings of postulated history, abandoned hunting and gathering, began to sing of the erotic strictures laid upon Nature by the cultivation of fields.

It was to Hamburg that he returned for the occasion of his final concert, the rescission of his career; not to Chez Poliphile, which had long been both extinguished and demolished, not to the bitter streets of the Inner Harbor, but to the Opera House itself, center of belief in the perdurability of culture. And there, with his companions of the voyage behind him, he returned to the water bittern, to a whole group of melodious birds excited by syncopation; at the intermission the conversation glittered with intensity. After it, he sang a group of mammals, made briefer by the requirements of his intention, his closing accomplishment.

It began in the ultimate reaches of the East, in unnamed places before the habit of geography had penetrated the primate mind. It wandered through delicately increasing recognitions, the I, the you, the community of we. It made its way from blood into the birth of worship, approaching relentlessly, an express train of a perception, all noise and motion, to the consciousness of Hamburg, the world poised between the wars without knowing that it was poised, without comprehending the nature of its destiny. But throughout the gilt and crimson auditorium there grew a sense of intolerable excitement.

The Troll King left the stage for a moment and then returned to conclude the evening's entertainment, dressed, to the wonder of the audience, in a tailcoat of perfect gloss, such as might be worn to receive a benediction from the King of Sweden. A tailcoat, a white tie as if a living butterfly had condescended to join him, ebony cane and ebony top hat reflecting icily the lights of the theatre. As he sang, the group behind him assisted. The drummer's hairy hands contracted themselves, pounding on the resonance of a high-hat cymbal. Sister One elevated herself on one leg, her flute dipping beaklike to a sheet of fruitful water; Sister Two made honey drip, particle by slow harmonious particle, into an organized comb. The music climbed and ended; almost before it ended, a weeping gorilla in the first row of the audience led the applause.

Hootali Ajignat

Do these words mean what I assume they mean?
Is there a man hootali thinking ajignat
or is there a mountain they are both climbing
being alternately the one climbed upon and the one climbing?

I am trying to work, here, under the dropcloths
representing the end of the world, with a machine
defined not as its shape but as its function.
In motion, I am that motion; out of motion
only a readiness. Not the house
that the gingerbread witch lives in and bakes and eats.

I think it is right in adolescence to believe in God
because we have to live in family and God is family.
But family falls away, towns disappearing
behind the moving train, then the train itself
becoming more skeletal until it is a hollow
train-shaped space moving in the space around it.

If I am that machine increasingly,
hootali and ajignat are manipulable.
It calls for the most careful exercise
of responsibility: to paint them without paint,
respecting the possibility that they could be painted.

Alas, children, you calling at Hallowe'en
in the guise of spirits, I have no physical gifts,
no candy skulls, no bitter chocolate coffins.
The end of the world is beyond death, death being a body.
The end of the world is irreversible, this machine
arranging itself to be and be in tomorrow.

Large and Begrudging

The Mercator projection, Greenland bigger than it is in life. Preference given to the ice, the ice as a rectangle. Over it the surveying party makes its way, Captain Blood and his henchmen, the tents carried by syphilitic natives. A subaltern goes mad, begins firing his Lee-Enfield in the direction of the ice mirages. Incapable of being understood when it is squared. They stand as in a hologram, alive only when viewed from the one direction. Far behind them the sucking noise of cattle drawing their hooves from the mud at the stream's margin, the child at his mother's breast, invention and worldwide distribution of the vacuum cleaner, the Pope with an unintentional mouth noise kissing the soil of Brazil. Here on the right meridian their shoes melt, they walk naked, stamped with male copyrights, into the ice volcanoes. Nothing left of them by morning other than a general agreement that all of the procedures are in need of change.

The Bone Pit

1.

Roisterers drunk, cursing in the cheap
London ale-houses as the dead cart with its load
trundles by them, following it to the edge
of the bone pit as the bodies are tumbled in
on top of one another, half-clothed, naked, the flash
now and then of an earring the collectors
missed in their despoiling urgency, cursing the
idea of a God who could so depopulate
what he had constructed, no light but torches,
the night sky moonless and starless, sitting down
like a pot lid on its boiling.

2.

My sparrow, my dusky
instructed lover, it is the hour before Christmas,
when wanderers look for a place to give birth and are refused.
The doll with its china eyes is wrapped and gilded,
kneaded by Muzak™ to a malleable consistency,
popped into ovens and comes out with a glistening crust
for a great mouth under the East—this is our design.

3.

The girl left her father, priest
of a little country town, when the line of dancers
came down the road out of the wood, having given up
homes, children, food, having annihilated themselves
into the dancing. Her father ran after her,
seized her roughly by the arm, dragged. Her arm came off
and with her other hand she held the hand

of the dancer beside her and so bleeding
they disappeared dancing over a rise into the next country.

4.

In an ash country mud
gathers itself in its hot pool into a boil
and swells painfully toward the air, stretches
its dome thinner, with a sigh of mud satisfaction
bursts, collapses, and the swelling begins again.
Here is a place to begin dying.

God curses back, and he has the heaviest
balls to curse with: by my balls, he
curses, you loiterers on the edge
of the mushy lung-whistling pit, fall in, fall in,
in the name of my mutilation, in the names
of all the torn, in the blind name of tearing.

5.

Sister and brother animals, goat-
footed refugees of the rocks, climbing
terrified up out of the ruck of cities, a hoof
visible, an eye, what we have escaped with,
a set of pearl-handled fish knives, photographs
of our high school graduation, the air thinning
in the places where no one lives, sister and brother,

lover, my ill-sung lover, my mute sparrow,
my song in the cypress, the arm I clutch
under and over the mechanics of the dance,
under and over the bray of bottomless music,
how to alleviate you, where you go on two sticks
after the election, how to back off from
having been chosen?

6.

What they mean by dementia is not
madness, fury, only that the mind
skips, now and then, over what it thought
it knew was there, a doll unraveling
in a ward marked with an orange sign on the door
reading Blood Precautions.

In the next examining room "After what
I've been through these two years, I'm not going to try
any more medicine. I asked my priest.
He says that it's not a sin."

7.

A glass of water, half full, forming a prism
the sunlight glitters into, and is separated
into its residual colors, blue, yellow,
each of them worth looking at lovingly,
worth seeing for its own self, for what it is.
Here, while I am writing to you, it has become morning.
The angers of the little hours and their helplessness go away.
Time to let memory go, to become
a single note playing on the surface of the cold air,
cold enough to stiffen the little hairs
in your nose, to make breath evidence.

8.

Arms growing up out of the pit in twists
of leaf, all leaf, not the eye looking
over it and ordering, not the leaf
made for a purpose and drying into it.

One at a time he is
retrieved, she is, there is no they
about them, each
stoops to retrieve its own.

9.

Light before color becomes evident, the edge of light
that allows only shape, only the ability to know
there is a difference, an expectation in the darkness.
Staying there with the one, not
walking out to the conclusion of the adventure.

My dusky sea
sparrow, it is the winter of one
and the sleep of one, dying
by itself in praise of itself, as the light
forgets even to grow where the air enters.

Post-Modernism

Her name was Gretl, and after he had stripped the rags from her meager body, which showed the clinical effect of rickets in childhood, he iced her with plaster of Paris, a pale pink, almost the color of a faded baby, and placed her in the window under a drapery of light veiling, ready for the first day of the festival. He told her she commemorated the slaughter of the innocents, under Herod. She stood as still as knife-pleating; it was the first time her hairstyle had been important. Toward dawn the devout began to gather, shuffling all the way from the city gate to the pickle of saints on the sidewalk outside the cathedral, all the way on their bruised knees.

Spam

Spandrel. An area between the extradoses of two adjoining arches, or between the extrados of an arch and a perpendicular through the extrados at the springing line. The decoration occupying the corner of a stamp between the border and an oval or circular central design.

Spaghetti straps. Down the broad marble staircase from the loggia into the formal gardens. A glowing cigarette end thrown away, as if by his black tie. A train leaving for Tiflis in the early morning.

Spackle. A brand of quick-drying plasterlike material, for patching plasterwork.

Spain.

Spanking. Moving rapidly and smartly. Quick and vigorous, a spanking pace. But ahead of them a cul-de-sac, confusion registering at the heads of the horses, and then the man with the revolver stepping forward.

Sparge. To scatter or sprinkle. Through the tall gloom of the cathedral at Burgos, the bishop preceded by statues of Christ in colored wax, and the congregation crossing itself, perfumed with incense, sparged with the holy water.

Spark photography. Photography of fast-moving objects, as bullets, by the light of an electric spark.

Spark gap. A space between two electrodes, across which a discharge of electricity may take place. After her aunt, the countess, dies in her chair of fright. . . it is then that she climbs onto the parapet, throws herself into the Neva.

Sparrow grass. Asparagus, by folk etymology.

Sparring partner. A boxer who spars with and otherwise serves to train a boxer who is preparing for a bout. Also called sparring mate. Spits out the bloody mouthpiece.

Space stage. A stage set, often limited to an arrangement of ramps and platforms, in which actors and set pieces are spotlighted against the bare background of a dark or black cyclorama.

Spadework. Preliminary or initial work, such as the gathering of data, on which further activity is to be based.

Spam. The sound of the heavy guns, once again over the ruined marshes, sounding like meat beaten together. Spam. Spam.

Eleanor of Aquitaine, Marie of Champagne, Courtly Love and the Troubadours

First the King of France takes all of the holy images out of the
    convents and monasteries.
The images are melted down to pay for another crusade; the
    Pope has urged the King of France to crusade.
A crusade will free the Holy City of Jerusalem from desecration at
    the hands of the infidel.
It will keep the King of Jerusalem on his throne and serve as a
    severe moral rebuke to the impertinences of Saladin.

First the Count of Anjou builds six more border castles, taxing
    the villagers.
A border castle tax imposed on top of the crusade tax.
Richard the Lion-Hearted is retrieved from being held as hostage
    by Henry Hohenstaufen, the Holy Roman Emperor.
A hostage tax is imposed on top of the border castle tax.
All of the holy images of the convents and monasteries are melted
    down that were not melted down previously.
At Poitou Marie of Champagne is instructing the younger sons of
    the nobility in the niceties of the courts of love.
All of the younger sons are learning to dance and when not to
    spit into the ladies' cleavages.

When they are not learning they are trying to overthrow father,
    who has divorced mother on the convenient if specious
    grounds of consanguinity.
The archbishop is horrified and then martyred, an additional
    expense.
Over and over the villages are ravaged and the peasant women
    raped and their bodies ground into the increasingly unpro-
    ductive soil.

Four hundred pages of this and it is more than time for the intro-
    duction of double-entry bookkeeping.

It is time for a sensible pattern of crop rotation including the peri-
  odic use of alfalfa and soybeans.
It is time for the barons of England to force John Lackland into
  signing the Magna Carta,
time for ragged schools to begin to educate the children of pover-
  ty sleeping under Blackfriars Bridge.

There is much to be said for history, the most important thing to
  be said being that it is over.
Much to be said for Marie de Champagne and the courts of love,
  which have led almost directly into the contemporary
  motion picture.
Much to be admired in chivalry as soon as it is debarred as a prin-
  cipal mode of taxation.
Much to be sung, idly, in the courtyard of the community
  college, of the flea-bitten paranoid blood-colored
  troubadour, Bertran de Born.

III

THE EDUCATION OF DESIRE

My Sweet Undertaker: A Blues

Nobody makes me pretty like my sweet undertaker.
Nobody puts the mascara onto my eyelashes one by one.
Nobody waits the long night through with my lipstick.

I had a man who was real, body and bone real.
The blood pumped around in his veins as fast as whiskey.
The real ones leave, hump out of town on morning.

Nobody makes me pretty like my sweet undertaker.
Nobody puts the pads in my cheeks to make me plump.
Nobody fixes the little spit curls down with adhesive.

I had a husband hot as the Ace of Noon
and he took him and cut himself out in the cancer bedroom.
The real ones live too much where old Jack Scratch itches.

Nobody makes me pretty like my sweet undertaker.
Nobody lays me around with lily of the valley.
Nobody counts the sponges and remembers whose.

I had a baby boy all of my own and sturdy
and he grew up into his juices a traveling man.
The real ones can't stop even where the edge goes over.

Nobody makes me pretty like my sweet undertaker.
Nobody builds a bird nest into my hair.
Nobody whistles for a wind to strip me certain.

I had an old Big Daddy the size of Jerusalem
hold me in his hand like I was the root of evening.
I had them all: I drew to two Jacks and won.

Nobody makes me pretty like my sweet undertaker.
Nobody cries like he cries, so little and final.
Nobody shovels me under in the name of home.

The Death of John Berryman

Henry went over the edge of the bridge first; he always did.
Then Mr. Interlocutor and Mr. Bones, then the blackface min-
        strels
with their tambourines. You have to empty out
all of the contents before the person himself dies.

The beard went over the edge; and Stephen Crane,
and the never-completed scholarly work on Shakespeare,
and faculty wives, and a sheaf of recovery wards
white-taled in the blue shadow of the little hours.

He loosened his necktie and the recurrent dream
of walking out under water to the destined island.
His mother went over in pearls; his father went over.
His real father went over, whoever his father was.
He thought to go over with someone, hand in hand
with perhaps Mistress Bradstreet, but someone always preceded
        him.
The news of his death preceded him. It hit the water
with a fat splash and the target twanged.

When there was nothing to see with or hear with, the silent traffic
of bystanders wrapped in snow, his only body
let itself loose, turned and waved before it went over
to what it could never understand as being the human shore.

Roses

Five years of drought. This garden, never watered,
blooms regardless, tapping an underground stream
that used to surface in a lagoon where the Zen
bakery dispenses organic muffins. We take the new
electric hedge clipper and its bright blue 100-foot
extension cord to the front hedge and trim it back
into respectability, and with it fall
the pink roses, the floppy disreputable ones
that refuse to live indoors.

Somewhere behind us
on the eucalyptus hill, is Ishi's cave
where he went to be alone when life in his room
in the Anthropological Museum became too tiring.
Only the children in the neighborhood know where the cave is.

The nasturtium seeds we sprinkled out on the wet ground
keep returning out of the tangle of Himalayan blackberry.
A branch breaks off the plum tree with its weight of fruit.
Confusion of Easter lilies and fern. Suckers of ivy take back
the wall of the house next door where the painters
dispossessed them, and twenty feet up, orange, exuberant
in a pine tree, a single nasturtium displays itself.
Look, it says, did you think I could climb this far?

This has been a year of deaths: Allen Barnett
in a New York AIDS ward, leaving the body's dangers;
Sara Vogan alone in her room, Ann Fields
before a Pacifica altar after four years of dialysis,
Susan Skov teaching her classes until the last week.
We put on polite clothes and go to funerals.
Trumpet stop on the organ, Amazing Grace
flung by a black projector onto the white church wall.

It took us an afternoon working hard
with gloves and a battered garbage can and three pairs of shears

to cut back half of Cecil Brunner, the white climber
with nothing to climb on, that sprays itself
out and up, grabbing hungrily for
tree boughs, porch railings, insinuating itself
into the male camellia. Now, everywhere we cut,
the new red stems have pushed out into the December air
and their young thorns harden.

The tulip tree bloomed twice, and the flowering plum
on the front sidewalk, even though someone broke off
the boughs that projected into the street parking space
and laid them neatly to die at the tree's feet.
We shower less. Each month we have come in
well under our water allotment.

At night I go down the back stairs to the garden
first, with a flashlight, to see if the skunk roads
are free of traffic. Then Merlin goes down.
Then we shut up the house, and go to bed,
and all night the roses meditate on growing.

We are here. We hope you are well. We hope you hear
every night, in the dark, the small sound of underground water.

Evening

1.

Then it is evening and the upwelling flush
of Chinese vermilion makes of the placed clouds
and the snow mountains historic illuminations,
permanence in the moment, that seductive art.
The more seductive as the body's loud
thunder of impulses, passion of concentration,
loosens out to a thinner age, part image, part
space in between the feathery strokes of the brush.

The evening, then: to take, and to relinquish.
The mountains have the color of a thought
remembered for centuries, and then dismissed.
The lovers in love with what the moment brought,
even as the moment itself begins to vanish,
even as their lips answer to being kissed.

2.

The mountains have the color of a thought.
Between two things, being part of neither,
the cones and cubes of the day's geometry
gone, the diagram of stars not yet fulfilled.
Here, in the emptiness of if, of whether,
the mind eludes conditions of symmetry,
quiets in motion to an unbesought
fountain ceaselessly filling, ceaselessly spilled.

Making love by evening light, their shadows walk
above their bodies' nakedness to change.
They are no longer in themselves complete.
Day calls them: to incorporate tick and tock.
Night calls; they linger on the paling sheet,
halfway familiar yet, and halfway strange.

3.

The mind eludes conditions of symmetry.
From childhood building these offices to contain,
conclude, make boundaries between in and out,
(this careful footstep on this careful stair).
Evening undoes intention, the clouds spare
a message-space, on which no truths remain
intelligible, the heaviest mountains doubt
demonstrations of their sheer integrity.

Free into loss, the lovers, as they follow
the upper air, thinness beyond mere breath,
move and are moved, ambiguities of as
entering their words, death or a sexual death
leaving transparent on the hollow pillow
what has become other than it thought it was.

The Education of Desire

> To find one same source for all good and all evil is to
> insist on the need for the education of desire.
> —Allen Mandelbaum, introduction to Dante's *Purgatorio*

1.

The archipelago at first light strewn in cloud, low-lying fog, moving and shifting, sleep turns to waking, birds from their nothingness of night to being seen, inviting quality in the awakening human voice, white with allusions. Birds make their bickering crosses, their solstices of air, invent themselves and globes around themselves, spaces of music to flirt and occupy. In unknown air, at morning, *la naissance du jour*, wake into nakedness or the shape as mind touches itself forming toward nakedness, our first division, generative wilderness of sleep from day it generates, love nothingness shows the dear idea of body, what it, which can touch nothing, desires to touch. A bell rings in the breakers, the dead brought home through wrack from unremembering, was entering is, live body stretches, tests its calves, thighs, raises its arms in air, opens itself to air, fills with the history of birds, transparent messages of water.

2. Aubade

O
island whose
edge frills with
his hair's
networks

if
never waking you
sensual and indolent
could yourself hold
beyond night's lessenings
shape of
our sleep.

No:
up from stung sea
stone invigilators
wake, watch who we were and are,
air fills and overfills
with our given names.

3. *Margins*

In summer sunlight, noon of the hot square, we join the audi-
ence, watch the white nakedness of the male and female witches,
their body hair subdued, eyes looking past us into the experi-
enced rooms of their torture, being brought for execution. It is
our chance: to watch one thing teeter on the edge of itself, walk
back and forth along the imaginary precipice, before it swallows
its hot breath and hurtles into absence. We wear our holiday
clothes; the archbishop, face smooth and plump as a plum at the
height of ripeness, quiets his excited vestments. The stake, sedate
in its pile of straw, waits at the borderline, is expectation's coun-
try. Smell of mimosa and flesh, smoke from the censers, structure
of saints piled up one above another, open-mouthed and crystal,
all the believed-ins. As the first fire catches and flares, our breaths
come out of us like seed, spasms of seed, trying to reach where the
fire goes, and the eyes of the witch travel from left to right, white
to the exercises past white, unraveling beyond us.

4. The River Crossing

The barge is called semiotics; it rides low in the water, burdened
    with analysis and truth.
Enter it, little one, you whose hands and feet were deformed by
    thinking, it is native to you, it is your luck.
It is mathematically exact; the eyes painted on either side of its
    prow have already done your despairing.

Without steersman or oarsmen, it lifts to the black vein of the
    current, indifference modifying indifference.
There are others with you, commenting on the cruces of their
    experience as written.
Hands held flatly before their faces, the palm of each hand paper-
    white, glossed with the stigmata of text.

Who weeps at the humiliation of memory, the kittens and
    pinafores left uninvaded to clutter the floor of the nursery?
The breasts with their smear of milk, a childhood of peristalsis?
If the boundary between love and the glossary of love can be
    predicated, it can be reached.

The other shore is a crowd of engraved obelisks, coming down to
    the very edge, specific boundary, its understanding of what
    is not water.
A Sybil is wound up; choruses of cenobites join her in articulat-
    ing a seven-voiced fugue of greeting.
The boat beaches as if recognizing the sign, absolute, for home.

5.

Immense I under
your weight of love
labor to be human.

The dove does
what its plume dictates the
ordained mounting.

I take you up as
mysterious as breath
in the spilt morning

who will not
arrange yourself, are
beyond hurry

casting your flesh as a
net thrown over
the node of water

asks recognition for
what it contains,
what passes through it.

The sun sees
what it shines on
and makes meaning.

Here is the hard
rib-cage the knife
knows and belongs to,

blood in my kiss,
broad-sounding bell
that your bone enters.

6. Woodland

Corydon playing his flute, the sheep arranged, a matinée of
dowagers indoctrinated from childhood, reading the next lace
number from the familiar program. Phyllis on point, her pirou-
ettes the exact little pattern of the blue hills, their trees neatly
pumiced and pollarded. How the sun shines once it has been
carefully pasted to the middle heaven! Radicchio and tiny aspara-
gus out of season, quail eggs and napkins folded in the shapes of
swans, a conception more intricate than luncheon, the gauze

scrim lifts to illuminate. Afterwards we all lounge on the incurious grass, posing for smocked painters. The last radish. No perception of time passing; if it is last it will be last forever. Surveyors roll in carts with heavy subversive masks of tragedy and comedy, setting them humming at either side of the clipped stage. A grid descends over us and a brush begins to paint by numbers, filling in the easy outlines of the untroubled sheep.

7.

Corms, tubers, dry
diagrams of what
under the restless spring
is to be got.

Seed in seed-
channel where the old lips
fold back in lubrication
and life slips

out from between them into
moist giving dirt.
Bulbs, syllables, all
those extrovert

loves flowers & mimicries sprung
out of compressed race
into exploded song
seeking its wide space.

8.

I was among the company that lost its way, advancing from the ships at Vera Cruz to mount the track toward the City of Mexico, of which we had heard much, and all a marvel. We had our horses and our helms, those signs of pre-eminence of which the unsaved stood in awe, and our white faces, the purity with which God recognized our holy nation. We rode as sculptures might, straight through the railings of the civic square into ordinary appearance, where we could not be understood. Silk of our banners punctuating the high air, and in our nostrils the odorous smoke of common sacrifice.

In the mountains we could no longer ride. Trails narrowed, the map of the country ceased to live in our minds, becoming, moment by dissolving moment, the shape of river and forehead, hand and embroidered leaf. We stopped when we reached the village and made ourselves into signs, stepping to our remembered places: the sign of the shield, with the many eyes of God, and the mouth of God open at its center; the sign of the rust-red cross with its centuries of passionate invitation. The signs glittered by themselves in the steep blue. There was no language.

I remember when she first unlocked me, a dwarf that had lived all its life in a cage of its own dimensions, a soft thing held like a multi-pointed tent on a forest of crutches. I could not believe in the vulnerability of my design, all fingers and hair and ears, all thin peninsulas, incapable of fortification. My flesh shook on my skeleton, dancing, with its own bewildering interplay of will and motion. I became half her, as a saint mates with its waiting shadow.

Pages of a journal, watercolors of umber and chocolate, the unfamiliar fruit piled in its colors of earth and innerness, spilling its delicacy out as the sutures ruptured. The houses earth, coaxed, as one tames a child, into the shapes of houses. Veins of the stream into the red irrigation of my body. Became the eye of a bird, as round as its round horizon, looking earthward, and the earth looking up from our jungle of public mounds, from our sweat and mountains.

9.

Arguing, in a cell of the old library, before the loss of faith and
   the subsequent invasion.
Philosophy told us our shapes: that we had two shapes, a left

shape of organized fire, and a right shape of porous, receptive lead.

And that we had two numbers, our number by night being a multiple of our number by day, but untranslatable.

Bilaterality was the plan of the living being, opening from its spine like the matched pages of a book having only the two pages.

Prophets on fire in the marketplace said we are everywhere in the imagination, but we knew better than to believe them.

Our child's game: one hand strikes and the other hand cups to receive it.

Our doors open or shut; the idea governing a door cannot be otherwise.

So we spoke, you and I, exchanging the sides of the board and the two colors of the conventional antagonists.

I learned and then you learned, and while you were learning I forgot, but was eager to learn again when my time came.

The invaders were not, as we had expected, material: lean nomads on flea-bitten horses.

They were forgettings: a brick forgotten in the wall and the wall fails to respond to its definition,

a voice forgotten in the choir and the music trails off into incoherence.

The invaders belonged to night, to a starless night, to an altar of night dedicated to incomplete prayers of forgetting.

Each of us supposed it was the other's turn to dream: alternation escaped us.

I saw you with the lower half of your face intact and your eyes missing; I could not for the life of me call to mind what had been the color of your eyes.

10. Earthquake, Volcano

Love, here are cherries picked from the ripe tree,
summer in a basket of porcelain, they lie

ready to the lip washed with their own color,
catching the eye.

Here is the wine of winter, captured in glass
so that in sorrow's time it can speak of pleasure,
loosening your body until your cold responsibilities pass
into dreams of leisure.

All of the food and drink, love, the tastes I offer
are of what first was here, of what then is missing,
love being always the music recapturing for you
your first kissing.

Neither the body clenched, nor the body after,
neither the wave's curling height, nor the trough that hollows,
only their color in time, the experienced sky
and its fleet swallows.

11. *Promenade des Anglais*

> We danced at the Chateau de Madrid. The Spanish King
> brushed past us, eating salted almonds.
> > —Michael Arlen, *The Green Hat*

Burying the dead, the dog walks draped in black behind the twin
      perambulator.
Life is lace and goffering irons, love gains weight in the heap of its
      paraphernalia.

All of the ideas of the ancients have rained down onto this exact
      spot
and been transformed to goods: Wellington boots, indelicate
      cameos of Bacchus.

The Bishop arrives in a catamaran made out of balsa wood
in which he has traced the migrations of Polynesians across the
      Pacific.

Clocks bulge with hours; there are seven courses on the hotel's
     luncheon table.
In the bedroom, the ravenous gape of the ivory hair collector.
We speak with doubtfulness of the far blue shadow of the African
     shore,
and of our fathers and uncles, who may be studying evolution.

All day and all night the conversation circles upon itself.
As one promenader dies, another emerges from her loosed reticule.

We lament in whispers the shadow side of love, labor, the bloody
     child
dropping into the air naked, an animal's means of communication.

For tea there will be iced *petits-fours*, mushroom sandwiches,
     langues de chat.
The slight tide of the middle of the collected earth tongues at the
     breakwater.

12.

On the white road
in dust of summer
someone's arriving

apricots bend
from the wall-garden
welcoming summer

someone's arriving
clothed only in light
his hands empty

his eyes full of islands
stroked by blue ocean
in the summer air

violent and singing
on the empty road
someone's arriving

the white light
cherishing his step
and his naked stare.

ACKNOWLEDGMENTS

The poem "The Arrival of the Titanic" first appeared in POET-RY, © 1995 by The Modern Poetry Association, and is reprinted by permission of the Editor of POETRY. This poem has also appeared in *Best American Poetry 1996*.

"The Death of John Berryman," which first appeared as a broadside from Hit and Run Press of Lafayette, California, and subsequently in POETRY, © 1996 by The Modern Poetry Association, is reprinted by permission of the Editor of POETRY.

"The Quest for the Holy Grail," "Had I Been the Virgin Mary I Would Have Said No," "Moons," "David Dances Before Saul," and "Tribe from the Interior," are reprinted by permission of *Indiana Review*, which holds copyright.

"Chants" and "My Sweet Undertaker: A Blues" first appeared in a special book edition of *Bastard Review, #5/6, death and desire*.

"The Metamorphoses" appeared as a chapbook from Senex Press in San Francisco.

Sections VIII and XII of *The Education of Desire* are reproduced by permission of *The Carolina Quarterly*.

Other poems in this collection have previously appeared in *Antioch Review, Barnabe Mountain Review, Blue Unicorn, The Bread Loaf Anthology of Contemporary Poetry, Chelsea, Colorado North Review, Denver Quarterly, Five Fingers Review, James White Review, Liberty Hill Poetry Review, Seneca Review,* and *The Southern Review*.